Amber
4/291
1/91
8.50

T⬛⬛⬛⬛ &
DRINKING FOUNTAINS

Philip Davies

TROUGHS & DRINKING FOUNTAINS
Fountains of Life

Chatto & Windus
LONDON

Published in 1989 by
Chatto & Windus Ltd
30 Bedford Square
London WC1B 3SG

A CIP catalogue record for this book
is available from the British Library

ISBN 0 7011 3369 4

Photoset and printed in Great Britain by
Redwood Burn Limited, Trowbridge, Wiltshire

CONTENTS

To J.E.D.
My Spiritual Mentor

KNOW THYSELF

Whosoever drinketh of the water that I shall give him
shall never thirst
(John 4.14)

By water everything lives.
(The Quran)

PREFACE

The purpose of this book is to draw attention to a long-neglected aspect of architectural and social history. Little has ever been written on the subject and, until now, no attempt has been made to survey the fascinating range of architectural forms and styles which were employed.

The book is not intended to cover ornamental fountains, however splendid these may be, but concentrates on those drinking fountains, pumps and wells which provided a basic daily need for countless towns and villages all over Britain. In particular it examines the role of the Metropolitan Drinking Fountain and Cattle Trough Association and the work of similar philanthropic bodies in alleviating conditions for the poor in nineteenth-century England.

It is my earnest hope that readers who are interested will press their local councils to ensure that surviving drinking fountains, pumps, troughs and wells are accorded proper consideration, and that effective measures are taken to secure their repair and long-term conservation. Even utilitarian wall fountains tell us a great deal about the social preoccupations of former generations and the sanitary conditions of the time, as well as being charming items of street furniture which add interest and character to the local scene. Unless public opinion is mobilised in this way, a unique part of the national heritage could be lost forever.

FOUNTAINS OF LIFE

'The Fear of the Lord is A Fountain of Life'. Inscriptions like this, carved on a Victorian Gothic drinking fountain in Lincoln's Inn Fields, epitomise the evangelical piety associated with the moral crusade for sanitary reform in mid-Victorian England. The provision of free, fresh drinking water was one of the most pressing social issues of the nineteenth century, not just in the capital, but across a country undergoing unprecedented population growth, where local Boards and vestries grappled with a totally inadequate sanitary infrastructure.

The noble fight for sanitary reform is well-documented in both literature and history. But the story cannot be reduced to a simple political or social struggle between enlightened, humanitarian promoters of government intervention and collectivism on the one hand, and jealously-guarded, vested interests infused with popular doctrines of *laissez-faire*, on the other. In reality the process was far more complex.

Philanthropic bodies and civic amenity groups played a significant and sometimes crucial role in advancing sanitary improvements from the 1850s onwards. Foremost among such organisations was the public drinking-fountain movement, which was notable for mobilising the support of prominent public figures, and for its practical contribution in providing hundreds of free public drinking fountains to alleviate conditions for the urban poor.

Historically London's water supply had always proved difficult. Mediaeval London, bounded by the Fleet in the west and the Walbrook in the east, drew 'sweet and fresh' waters from a natural network of springs and streams. William Fitzstephen, writing in

1180–82, speaks of London's suburbs having 'most excellent wells, whose waters are sweet, wholesome and clear.' Generally these were natural springs, and several, such as Clerkenwell and St Clement's well, were considered holy, but they were isolated sources. Most residents drew water from the Thames, or from the Fleet, Walbrook, Langbourn and Oldbourne (Holborn), but by the thirteenth century these had become contaminated open sewers. Demand outstripped fresh sources of supply.

John Stow records that in 1236 'the citizens were forced to seek waters abroad.' The result was the construction of the Great Conduit, financed by French merchants, which conveyed water from Tyburn to the City along the present line of Oxford Street, Holborn and Cheapside. From here water was distributed underground in bored-elm pipes, varying between two to ten inches wide, to a system of pumps and cisterns, with quills of lead carrying water to the houses of the wealthier nobles and merchants. When Edward I returned from the Holy Land in 1274 it is alleged that 'the Conduit in Chepe ran all day with red and white wine.'

By the reign of Edward III supplies had become totally inadequate for their purpose. In the fifteenth century a number of public benefactions were given for the repair and restoration of water supplies to the capital. For instance, in 1437 John Pope, citizen and barber, willed his estates for the upkeep of city conduits. Four years later the City Corporation granted 1,000 marks for building and restoring conduits, as a result of which a considerable number of new ones were constructed. In 1471 further supplies were brought in from Paddington, and in 1479 the Great Conduit was rebuilt and enlarged. With the growth of London a much wider network of conduits was built to bring in water from outlying districts. By the close of the sixteenth century there were at least sixteen serving London.

One which conveyed supplies from a Pentonville spring to the Charterhouse is commemorated by White Conduit Street. Another, built by Sir William Lamb in Great Ormond Street in 1577, served the Oldbourne (Holborn) Cross and is recalled by Lamb's Conduit Street, Holborn. The Chimney or Devil's conduit was a fourteenth-century conduit head which was removed only in 1913. Situated at the rear of No. 20 Queen Square in Holborn, it augmented the supply to the Bloomsbury White Conduit, which stood in Chapel Street. Both supplied the Greyfriars monastery (later Christ's Hospital) in Newgate Street. The conduit was re-erected in 1924 behind the offices of the Metropolitan Water Board in Rosebery Avenue, where it still survives. Most other early conduits were destroyed by the Great Fire of 1666.

In the City of London guilds played an important role in providing public facilities. At Little Conduit, beside old St Paul's, wooden buckets were filled and collected by water carriers, who belonged to one of London's most prestigious guilds, the water-bearers. Many guilds operated their own pumps, wells or cisterns. Often these were elaborate ornamental structures. For instance, one in the yard of the Leather Sellers' Hall near Bishopsgate was enriched with a profuse array of grotesque ornament, and crowned by a voluptuous maiden from whose ample breasts wine flowed on public holidays. Another more chaste example was the sixteenth-century Aldgate Pump at the junction of Leadenhall Street and Fenchurch Street, rebuilt in 1871 as a pedimented stone pillar with vermiculated stone bands and a splendid brass spout in the form of a hound's head. In the City the Standard Conduit at Cornhill was the central point of measurement for all milestones from London.

Other cities had similar arrangements. Southampton had four conduits supplying the city. In 1567 Maidstone, for instance, appointed two wardens of the High Street conduit to collect charitable offerings for its upkeep.

In 1552 the first waterworks in the capital were built by a Dutchman, Peter Morrys – a colossal waterwheel built in to the arches of London Bridge to raise water from the Thames. This system, inaugurated under a five-hundred-year lease from the City Corporation, was extended as time went on until five of the arches

of the bridge were occupied with waterwheels. These supplied the
City for over 240 years and came to an end only with the
demolition of the old bridge in 1822. On average some 1,500,000
gallons a day were raised in this way. Later, in the seventeenth
century, the Fleet river was dammed to create a reservoir at
Hampstead Ponds. But these major feats of civil engineering were
eclipsed by the construction of the remarkable New River, a canal
nearly thirty-nine miles long, from Amwell and Chadwell in
Hertfordshire to Islington.

The New River was an open channel, 10 feet wide and 4 feet
deep, built along the 100-feet contour line from the Chadwell spring
to the New River Head at Islington, augmented at various points by
deep wells. Opened in 1613, it was built by Sir Hugh Myddleton
(1560–1631), a friend of Sir Walter Raleigh, and an energetic Welsh
entrepreneur and goldsmith totally untrained in engineering skills.
Myddleton, who is commemorated by a large memorial drinking
fountain on Islington Green (see p. 39), constructed a sophisticated
gravitational system of water supply that was to serve London from
the New River Head for over two hundred years. Initially the new
supply was connected to the existing network of conduits, but later
company street pumps were built, three of which are preserved in
the Guildhall Museum.

Domestic supply was always inadequate. Before the seventeenth
century applications for permission for a quill (the size of a goose
quill) of water to individual houses were often declined or ignored.
Where it was provided, water was laid through lead pipes to
basement storage cisterns. It was then pumped up to other cisterns
to give a head to water closets. These had been invented at the close
of the sixteenth century and were commonplace by the eighteenth
century, but their need for ample quantities of water greatly
increased the problems of both domestic supply and waste.

In the eighteenth century the development of steam pumps
provided new opportunities to draw water from the Thames, but as
a source the river was grossly polluted. Tobias Smollett wrote that

'Human excrement is the least offensive part of the concrete which is composed of all the drugs, minerals and poisons used in mechanics and manufacture enriched with the putrefying carcasses of beasts and men; and mixed with the scourings of all the washtubs, kennels and common sewers within the bills of mortality.'

By the early nineteenth century London's water supply was vested in the hands of nine private companies. These were the New River in North London, the Chelsea, West Middlesex and Grand Junction companies in West London, the East London waterworks, and the Southwark, Vauxhall, Lambeth and Kent companies in South London. The water they supplied was totally inadequate for the needs of the population, badly contaminated and responsible to a great degree for the fearfully high mortality rate.

Fortunes were made from the supply of polluted water, as these competitive companies vied with each other in the scramble for profits. It was not uncommon to find three separate companies supplying water to the same street of West End houses, whilst in poorer neighbourhoods supply was intermittent, inadequate and, more often than not, completely lacking. In 1811 competition was transmuted by an agreement between the companies into a geographically-based monopoly, fostering complacency, inefficiency and fiercely-guarded captive markets of long-suffering consumers.

Between 1800 and 1850 the population of London rose from 1,100,000 to 2,700,000, without any great investment in the sanitary infrastructure required to support such a growth. As the teeming rookeries became further overcrowded, cholera, typhoid, the white plague (TB) and typhus cast a necrophagous shadow over the capital.

Urban life was a nightmare for the poorer classes. Until the 'Sanitary Idea' promulgated by reformers such as Edwin Chadwick and Southwood Smith began to make headway in the 1850s, the concept of environmental health was as alien to Victorian minds as the connection between dirt and disease. Often the narrow alleyways and passages of the city were rendered impassable by accumulated piles of dirt and excrement. Dust heaps and middens the size of four-storey houses were commonplace nuisances.

It is difficult to exaggerate the appalling squalor of the Victorian city. Dr Hector Gavin visited Bethnal Green in the 1840s. He reported that a new terrace of houses had been constructed within ten feet of 'an enormous ditch or stagnant lake of thickened putrefying matter, containing dead dogs and cats in every stage of decomposition', from which 'bubbles of pestilential exhalation' were given off. It took men of the calibre of Henry Mayhew and Charles

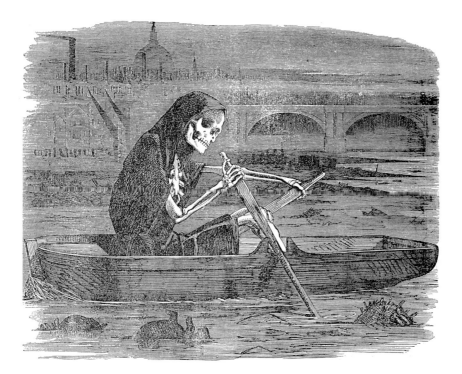

Tenniel's cartoon for *Punch* depicting the atrocious condition of the River Thames.

Dickens to convey to the public at large the horrifying depths of human degradation in which vast sections of the urban poor were trapped.

The explosive growth of London's population found the capital's water supply in a reprehensible condition. Although the Thames was little more than a sluggish current of effluent which reeked in hot weather, many water companies persisted in obtaining supplies from the very point at which the sewers debouched their contents into the river. A pamphlet of 1827 demanded:

> The water taken up from the River Thames between Chelsea Hospital and London Bridge, for the use of the inhabitants of the Metropolis, being charged with the contents of more than 130 public common sewers, the drainings from the dung-hills and lay-stalls, the refuse of hospitals, slaughter houses, colour, lead gas and soap works, drugs-mills and manufactures, and with all sorts of decomposed animal and vegetable substances, rendering the said water offensive and destructive to health, ought no longer to be taken up by any of the Companies from so foul a source.

The more fortunate relied on the old mediaeval system of conduits, wells and pumps, but these were not only inadequate, with one shared between 13,000 people in part of St Pancras for instance, but often as grossly polluted with impurities as river water. After an analysis of wells in the City of London in 1866 the Medical Officer wrote that

> In many cases the constituents are remarkably indicative of the source of the pollution. The wells of the meat markets are charged with the peculiar filth of those localities ... The wells of the City Churches are also strongly tainted with saltpetre and ammonia, doubtless the final product of the decay of the animal matter buried in the neighbouring graveyards.

Relatively few of these earlier communal pumps have survived, but two remain at Queen Square and Bedford Row in Holborn (see p.

40), embellished with Jacobean strapwork designs and crowned by
lanterns. An attractive Gothic pump can be found in Gray's Inn,
and a well is mentioned in the annals of Lincoln's Inn as early as
1509. A simple nineteenth-century stone pump still survives there in
the Great Court. Others remain in the City of London as
ornamental items of street furniture. In the West End there are two
interesting early nineteenth-century cast-iron pumps at Bryanston
Square and Montagu Square. Both take the form of fluted Doric
columns to match the entrance doorcases on the surrounding
houses.

More commonly people relied on their own rainwater butts,
communal standpipes and itinerant water sellers. Many simply
scooped water straight from the river or the gutters. The capital's
water supply was a national disgrace, which *Punch* exposed
ruthlessly when it commented on the Great Exhibition of 1851 –
'whoever can produce in London a glass of water fit to drink will
contribute the rarest and most universally useful article in the whole
exhibition.'

If any one incident was responsible for the growth of the
movement to supply free fresh drinking water to the indigent poor,
it was the cholera epidemic of 1849. Cholera, like plague, was a
sensational disease, shocking and degrading in its effects, but above
all, as it hit all classes of people, it acted as a catalyst on public
opinion which drove the petty parochialism of the complacent
vestries and water companies before it. The cholera outbreaks of
1847 and 1854 killed over 58,000 people in London alone, and the
angst with which it was regarded nurtured religion alongside
radicalism. A contemporary handbill read: 'Ought we not to view
the late fatal disease ... as a direct visitation of the Almighty? Were
not the first victims of Cholera, Drunkards, Bull-baiters and
characters of that description.'

The common belief that cholera was a miasmatic vapour
transmitted by foul air was dealt a fatal blow in 1854 when Dr John
Snow traced the source of an outbreak in Soho to the Broad Street

pump. One of the largest epidemiological investigations ever undertaken reported conclusively that the disease was waterborne, but it was not until 1883 that Robert Koch isolated the comma bacillus that caused the disease.

The problem of adequate supply recurred throughout the nineteenth century. In many ways it was exacerbated by the action of some Medical Officers and public authorities who closed down polluted public wells. To the public, well water often appeared pure as it was cool. In 1866 Dr Henry Letheby, the Medical Officer of Health for the City, recommended that none of the thirty-five pumps and five wells in the City be used for drinking. Where warning notices were ignored, pump handles were locked.

The daily problem of obtaining water created long queues at small public taps and standpipes, where supplies were intermittent. Given the difficulty of obtaining water for drinking purposes after a long and gruelling working day of twelve or fourteen hours, 'the minor comforts of cleanliness', wrote Edwin Chadwick in 1842, 'are of course foregone, to avoid the immediate and great discomforts of having to fetch water.' If the problem was bad in London, it was parlous in the new industrial towns of the north. One Lancashire collier said he never washed his body; he let his shirt rub the dirt off, though he hastened to add 'I wash my neck and ears and face, of course.'

By 1859 several provincial cities enjoyed the luxury of a constant water supply, but Sir John Simon's aim of an unrestricted supply for London 'as the first essential of decency, of comfort and of health' remained unfulfilled, although there had been major improvements.

With the introduction of the Metropolis Water Act of 1852 sanitary legislation assumed the novel virtue of an imperative stance. A Water Examiner, Sir Francis Bolton, was appointed for London. Filtration systems were enforced on all water supply companies. All reservoirs within five miles of St Paul's were instructed to be covered. Intakes from the Thames were relocated to the non-tidal areas above Teddington Weir. In 1855 the Metropolitan

Management Act created a two-tier system to oversee sanitary issues in the capital. A year later the Southwark Company was forced to move its source of supply on the Thames from below the main sewage outfall.

Ironically one result of this wave of reform was that conditions actually got worse when the Consolidated Commission of Sewers flushed out all its underground sewers straight in to the Thames. In 1858 matters reached a head with 'the Great Stink', a smell so pungent that the plans were made to evacuate the House of Commons to Hampton Court, a move that was only averted by heavy summer rains which restored a semblance of normality. *Punch* berated the city authorities with its cartoon 'Dirty Father Thames':

> Filthy river, filthy river,
> Foul from London to the Nore,
> What art thou but one vast gutter,
> One tremendous common shore?

> All beside thy sludgy waters,
> All beside thy reeking ooze,
> Christian folks inhale mephitis,
> Which thy bubbly bosom brews.

From the mid-century water supplies were monitored regularly by chemical and microscopic analysis. Public authorities became more vigilant and active in the fight to secure a minimum standard of purity. The impact was immediate. As soon as the Lambeth Water Company moved its intake up-river, the annual death rate in the area dropped from 130 to 37 per thousand. Supply remained a problem as water companies persistently refused to provide a constant flow. Until late in the century in many districts water was available only for limited hours of the day. Generally the poorer the district, the shorter the period.

At this point the philanthropic endeavours of the public drinking-fountain movement began to make serious headway. The initial impetus came not from London, but from the great non-conformist strongholds of the north, where urban reform was equated with a drive for greater cleanliness and sobriety. Here in the new industrial cities the rising middle classes expressed their new-found confidence and wealth in projects designed to foster civic pride.

In Liverpool the Corporation had secured extensive sanitary powers in 1847, including the ability to buy out water companies and to construct its own sources of supply. The provision of the first public baths in Britain was followed by philanthropic public drinking fountains erected in co-operation with the City Corporation. Other cities such as Hull, Derby and Bolton soon followed suit.

In October 1858 Charles Melly read a paper to the Liverpool meeting of the National Association for the Promotion of Social

left   An early fountain in the Liverpool Docks.
right   An early wall fountain erected in Chester.

Samuel Gurney, founder of the Metropolitan Free Drinking Fountain Association.

Science, recording the careful work which had been carried out in the city. It provoked national interest and was rapidly taken up by Samuel Gurney, MP for Penrhyn and Falmouth.

As a nephew of Elizabeth Fry, Gurney was endowed with a philanthropic zeal which his banking connections enabled him to fulfil. On 12 April 1859 he founded the Metropolitan Free Drinking Fountain Association in conjunction with an enthusiastic barrister, Edward Thomas Wakefield. The first meeting was held at Willis's Rooms in King Street under the chairmanship of the Earl of Carlisle, who became the first President. The inaugural meeting resolved

> That, whereas the erection of free drinking fountains, yielding pure cold water, would confer a boon on all classes, and especially the poor, an Association be formed for erecting and promoting the erection of such fountains in the Metropolis, to be styled 'The Metropolitan Free Drinking Fountain Association', and that such contributions be received for the purposes of the Association. That no fountain be erected or promoted by the Association which shall not be so constructed as to ensure by filters, or other suitable means, the perfect purity and coldness of the water.

Ironically it was the big brewery families of Hanbury and Buxton which became stalwarts of the new Association rather than the temperance societies, which initially viewed it with distrust.

The first fountain was opened amid scenes of public rejoicing on 21 April 1859 (see p. 41). Situated in the boundary railings of St Sepulchre's Church, Snow Hill, it was paid for entirely by Samuel Gurney. The opening ceremony by the daughter of the Archbishop of Canterbury was recorded for posterity by the *Illustrated London News*. The original Norman-style fountain was described: 'In a recess hewn out of the churchyard wall two small pillars are fixed, from the top of which springs a semi-circular arch, neatly moulded;

the sides of the recess, with the arch itself, are of polished Aberdeen granite. In the centre is a tastefully wrought shell of white marble, also highly polished.'

In 1867 the fountain was dismantled to allow the construction of the nearby Holborn Viaduct, but in 1913 it was reinstated in a modified form. The frieze is still inscribed 'The First drinking-fountain' over the name of the donor and the words 'Replace the Cup'. It is one of the few which retains its original cup and chain. Later, in the interests of public hygiene, most were replaced by upward jets of water.

Within a short space of time the fountain was used by over 7,000 people per day. In an initial burst of optimism the Association envisaged close co-operation with the local vestries and authorities in obtaining suitable sites and providing a fresh supply of water, but it rapidly ran into a wall of bureaucratic obtuseness. By 1865 over eighty-five fountains had been built, but many vestries declined to co-operate on the grounds that additional charges would be levied on local rates, or that 'such erections in the public streets would lead

The opening of the first free drinking fountain in London at St. Sepulchre's, Snow Hill on 21 April 1859, as depicted in the *Illustrated London News*.

to frequent obstructions of the traffic.' In some districts the Association had to remain content with providing fountains, but paying for the water from its own revenue. Together with the provision of loan after loan, this proved to be an enormous financial burden which nearly brought the Association to an untimely end. Even worse, in 1863 the Secretary absconded with several hundred pounds, and it was only through the munificence of Samuel Gurney that the Association managed to survive.

Gradually the more recalcitrant authorities were drawn into line. In 1870 the City Corporation set an important example when it voted £1200 for a new fountain at Smithfield, and granted £50 for the annual supply of water.

The origin of this particular fountain is interesting as it was funded by a bequest from Sir Martin Bowes, a former Lord Mayor of London in 1546, who left a sum of money for the repair of conduits in the city. The fountain, which still survives in a modified form, was designed by Francis Butler with a central bronze statue of 'Peace' crowned by a wheaten garland. Originally the statue was covered by an elaborate stone baldacchino with corner statues depicting Temperance, Faith, Hope and Charity, but this fell into disrepair. Only the centrepiece by J. Birnie Philip survives (see p. 42).

The location and siting of fountains tells us a great deal about the primary concerns of the Association – temperance and evangelism.

From its outset the Association was closely related to the temperance movement. Before the advent of the Association, the temperance societies were very active, but they offered no realistic alternative to the evils of drink. At this time tea and coffee were expensive luxuries beyond the reach of the working masses. It is hardly surprising that due to the lamentable inadequacy in both the distribution and condition of water the working masses preferred beer and spirits, even though the former was often laced with salt to exacerbate the thirst, or tobacco to give it colour, and the latter was frequently adulterated with vitriol. Faced with a stark choice

between water, which was hard to obtain and usually grossly contaminated, and ale or spirits, which were easy to come by, it is inevitable that many chose alcohol. Gin-drinking was widespread in eighteenth- and nineteenth-century England, its effects conveyed vividly in Hogarth's Gin Lane and other caricatures.

In some neighbourhoods chronic alcoholism was endemic. Whole families were sunk in sullen drunken squalor, their very addiction destroying what little chance they had of gainful employment or advancement. Some spent over a third of their income on drink. Given such an affront to human dignity, and the growing realisation that 'the absence of any ready alternative to the public house was the real evil to be removed', the Association led the movement to give the sober poor a fair chance of remaining so. Accordingly many fountains were sited deliberately close to popular public houses to offer the working man a character-building alternative to the evils of drink.

A good example opposite a public house can be seen in the wall of St Mary Abbot's Hospital in Kensington, inscribed with the morally uplifting verse:

Lord from Thy Blessed Throne
The Griefs of Earth look upon.
God Bless the Poor.
Make them from Strong Drink Free
Let their homes happy be
God Bless the Poor.

This strong moral dimension went hand in hand with the prevailing ethos of evangelical piety. Indeed the first paid secretary of the Association, John Matthias Weylland, saw the fountains movement as an opportunity to enlist wealthy aristocratic philanthropic support for his own evangelical work. This created considerable tension within the Association and eventually led to his dismissal, his fanatical proselytising having driven away potential contributors.

But the moral lesson of providing free fresh water for the suffering masses was one which lay deep in the Christian psyche, and scriptural allusions provide a recurrent theme in the location and form of many fountains. Some resemble baptismal fonts or carry apt quotations from the Bible. One of the most popular verses is inscribed on a wall fountain at Rosslyn Hill in Hampstead (see p. 43). It reads:

'Jesus said whosoever drinketh of this water shall thirst again but whosoever drinketh of the water I shall give him shall never thirst' (John IV 13:14)

Water was associated in the Christian tradition with purity of spirit and innocence. Therefore it is no coincidence that the most popular figures for public drinking fountains were either Biblical, such as the Woman of Samaria or Rebecca at the Well, or allegorical depictions of the spirits of Temperance and Charity, nor indeed that one of the most popular locations was the churchyard. Mediaeval romanticism inculcated nostalgia for a society where the church played a more central role in daily life. The association of pure fresh drinking water with the church was intended to foster a renaissance of

WHOSOEVER DRINKETH OF THE
WATER THAT I SHALL GIVE HIM
SHALL NEVER THIRST

High Victorian evangelism on an Association wall fountain.

spiritual values and to provide solace for the deprived urban poor at
the very place they would expect it most, binding the church once
more to the local community which it served.

By 1877 the Society's reputation was largely established and a
working relationship was obtained with most vestries. Early ridicule
of its efforts waned as influential patrons offered support,
culminating in a donation of £100 from Queen Victoria in 1877 for a
fountain and trough at Esher.

From its earliest days the Royal Society for the Prevention of
Cruelty to Animals recognised the value of the new Association. As
a result a large number of troughs were erected to provide free water

for cattle, horses and dogs, prompting the Association to change its name to the Metropolitan Drinking Fountain and Cattle Trough Association in 1867.

Owing to the activities of Commander Francis Anderson Calder RN (1787–1855), the city of Belfast set an early example in the provision of troughs for cattle and horses. As the founder of the Belfast Society for the Prevention of Cruelty to Animals, he erected ten troughs for the relief of animals in the city between 1843 and 1855. This forgotten idealist is commemorated by a large drinking fountain, now in Albert Square. By 1863 Belfast had twenty-one drinking fountains raised by the local Association.

In an age of motor transport it is difficult to visualise the acute suffering experienced by animals in nineteenth-century cities. It was commonplace for horses to be worked to death or for cattle to be driven to the great metropolitan markets on the hoof without water for two or three days in the height of summer. The Association wrote in 1872 that 'The sufferings which were endured by parched and wearied animals in our streets before the Society undertook the erection of cattle troughs ... must have been past all imagination'.

More than once the Association was accused of fostering Glanders disease with its communal troughs, but each time it was exonerated. By 1885 over 50,000 horses drank daily from London troughs alone – the filling stations of their day. Cabbies carried maps marked up to show the location of troughs throughout the city.

Early troughs were experimental in construction, and few of these have survived. Iron, which was used until 1870, proved too brittle, and timber with zinc lining was too vulnerable to everyday damage, so that granite was eventually adopted as the most durable material.

The provision of troughs was a shrewd move. It brought a substantial increase in revenue and the powerful support of the RSPCA. Moreover it enhanced support from the temperance societies as well, because many London publicans often provided communal troughs for patrons, but with a proviso that 'All that water their horses here must pay a penny or have some beer.'

As a voluntary society with limited funds, most of the troughs erected were straightforward utilitarian structures, and with the exception of a simple, chaste inscription, such as 'Be kind and merciful to all animals' or 'A righteous man regardeth the life of his beast', superfluous ornament was generally avoided.

The close relationship with the RSPCA is commemorated by a fine memorial drinking fountain outside Richmond Park with a corona of ornamental ironwork designed by T.E. Collcutt in 1891 to mark the anniversary of the Society's foundation (see p. 45).

A typical circular cast iron trough and fountain with hoof feet manufactured by Macfarlanes of Glasgow.

The great ironwork companies such as Macfarlane's produced large numbers of cast-iron cattle troughs as well as drinking fountains. Their catalogue depicts a range of sizes and types. One particularly popular type embodied a drinking fountain for human use with a circular horse trough carried on cast-iron horses' legs and hooves. A good example, complete with cast-iron 'hoof feet', survives in Essex alongside the main road to Harwich. A more simple early iron trough survives in London outside The Mason's Arms public house in Kensal Green.

The majority of troughs, though, were granite. Double troughs were quite common. Good examples survive in London at Albany Street outside the horse barracks (see p. 46), and in Park Crescent, Mornington Crescent, Goldington Crescent and elsewhere.

One of the more interesting is a small, single granite trough outside the Roundhouse in Chalk Farm which carries an inscription to Charles Kingsley, author of *The Water Babies*, who died in 1875. Another dedicated to his memory can be found in Hopton Street, Southwark. A delightful variation on the standard design occurs in Newcastle, where a roadside trough called the Cradle Well has a canopy at one end resembling a baby's cradle. Another more elaborate example, enriched with carved stonework and a boar's head stands outside The Fishmonger's Arms public house in Wood Green (see p. 47). Few are operational, most are neglected, and many have been converted to ornamental flower beds.

Some troughs were designed with a scrolled gable end and a curved bowl beneath to provide a simple facility for humans. A delightful survival can be found adjacent to the war memorial in Canterbury engraved with the inscription:

To our patient comrades of the Horse lines,
He paweth in the valley, he rejoyceth in his strength.

The verse commemorates the appalling losses of horses and men during the First World War. Perhaps the most poignant of all can be found far afield in Port Elizabeth, South Africa, where a splendid

Imperial memorial was raised by public subscription to recall the suffering of all animals killed in the Anglo-Boer War. It comprises a huge rough-hewn granite block with troughs and fountains surmounted by a full-size figure of a charger and a kneeling, helmeted soldier offering water to his horse. The President of the Memorial Trust wrote to the Association: 'The monument is splendid and commands respect ... and admiration. In a new country like this, to erect a monument to animals is a veritable triumph. The natives stand in utter astonishment before it.' It was inscribed with a prophetic Imperial epitaph:

> The Greatness of a Nation
> Consists not so much in the Number of Its People
> Or in the Extent of Its Territory
> As in the Extent and Justice of its Compassion.

As the Association consolidated, its image underwent a subtle but significant change. What had started out as a radical organisation, challenging the free market ethos of the private water companies and their monopoly of a necessity of life, gradually became a conservative charity run by retired generals and other establishment figures. In part this can be attributed to a weakening of evangelical non-conformism in the political arena, but it also reflected the changing nature and role of philanthropy in English life as the century wore on, and as local authorities increasingly provided basic civic amenities for the underprivileged.

With the change in the nature of the Association the design and form of the fountains tended to become more elaborate. Initially the Association had been anxious to ensure that functional utility was not sacrificed to ostentatious display, but gradually, as wealthy patrons commissioned their own fountains, design became more and more a paramount consideration, so that in time the Association's pattern book contained over one hundred and fifty fountains of the most exotic and flamboyant kind. This met with considerable aesthetic criticism. An article in *The Builder* of June 1864 remarked that 'It is unfortunately the case that the street fountains movement has not, upon the whole, been creditable to the taste or skill in design of the present generation.' Many were designed by Robert Keirle, who was consultant architect to the Association from 1858 to 1895, but others were designed by leading architects of the day.

In the mid-1850s, as the Association established itself, there was a flurry of interest in the design of drinking fountains. Design competitions were held and many entries were illustrated in journals like *The Builder*. For instance, in 1859 a range of Gothic designs by Henry Godwin were illustrated.

A plain utilitarian model was developed by the Association for standard use. This was free of all ornament and comprised a polished granite base, sometimes crowned by an urn, which could receive a simple carved dedication. But it is the more elaborate designs which are so interesting today – deliberately intended to flatter the vanity of the donor and to provide Art for the masses. As water sustained the body and cleansed the soul, so Art would elevate the spirit. As Howard Malchow has written, 'Fountains were part of everyday life, and while their water refreshed the body, their beauty nourished the spirit, and perhaps made the poor less brutish and less dangerous. Their message was one of temperance, religion, social peace and class collaboration: the poor and the peasant may meet to drink at the same fountain.'

Inevitably a large number of the most elaborate drinking fountains are found in London, where the work of the Association was concentrated. The City of London is particularly rich in the grandest examples. Two stand immediately behind the Royal Exchange. The earlier designed by J. Edmeston, an unusually refined composition with figures by Jules Dalou, was presented by the Drapers and Merchant Taylors' Companies through the Association in 1878 (see p. 48). The later of the two was erected to mark the Golden Jubilee of the Association in 1909, with fluted Ionic columns carrying a canopy over a bronze female figure (see p. 48). The motif of the female figure with a pitcher, common to many of the Association's drinking fountains, evoked the religious symbolism referred to earlier.

The figure recurs again on the Wills drinking fountain, transferred from the Royal Exchange to Blackfriars Bridge in 1911 (see p. 49). A most eloquent expression of commercial taste was embodied in a City fountain which was moved to Clapham Common in 1895 (see p. 50). Designed by Charles Barry for the United Temperance and General Provident Institution, it is a haunting memorial crowned by the poignant figures of a pleading woman offering succour to a crippled dying man.

The sheer variety of the designs is fascinating. A number consciously evoke Elysian idylls, such as that at Gloucester Gate, Regent's Park, with bronzework by Joseph Durham which takes the form of a female figure, Matilda, with a water pail crowning a cairn of stones (see p. 51). Pimlico Road boasts a fine flamboyant free Renaissance-style monument to the Second Marquess of Westminster with niches embellished with shell hoods and Cosmati work (see p. 52), whilst the side of the former St George's Hospital, Hyde Park Corner, sports a rococo shell basin beneath scrolled consoles (see p. 53).

Regent's Park was once graced by a monumental drinking fountain of two swans carrying an obelisk and female figure, recalling Diana and her swans from Greek mythology, but this was removed and sold in the mid-1960s. The splendid Greek Boy fountain in St James's Park, designed by C. H. Mabey in 1863, was badly vandalised in 1988, but it is now being repaired (see p. 54–5).

One of the most elegant of the smaller drinking fountains on the pastoral theme is in Old St Pancras churchyard (see p. 56). Based on the Choragic monument of Lysicrates in Athens, it is constructed in cast iron and takes the form of five fluted Corinthian columns on a circular plinth supporting a shallow dome and cherub. At Albert Gardens, off the Whitechapel Road, is a French cast-iron fountain of a shepherd boy complete with sickle, rake and wheatsheaf, strikingly at variance with its hard urban context (see p. 58). At

Hampstead Heath extension, by Wildwood Road, is an isolated Baroque Portland stone vase, set among the trees, redolent of some long-forgotten pastoral myth, offering ambrosia to the Gods (see p. 59).

One of the most delightful, without doubt, is near Marlborough Gate in Kensington Gardens, a small stone bowl and pedestal crowned by a bronze of two wrestling bears, erected to mark the eightieth anniversary of the Association in 1939 (see p. 60).

Holborn is also well endowed. Lincoln's Inn Fields has two – in the south-east and north-west corners. The former, a grand two-storey structure carrying a stone vase, commemorates the life of Philip Twells MP (see p. 61). The latter is smaller, carved with Gothic and Celtic motifs, and bears the inscription 'The Fear of the Lord is a Fountain of Life' (see p. 62), a quotation which recurs on the fountain outside the nearby St Dunstan's-in-the-West in Fleet Street (see p. 63).

Memorial drinking fountains and troughs became *de rigueur* in certain social circles. Many still survive, some to the famous, but more often as forgotten memorials to forgotten people.

One of the best preserved in London is at South End Green, Hampstead, erected in 1881 for a certain Miss Crump at Hereford House, in memory of her uncle (p. 64). Designed by J. H. Evins, it takes the form of a baptismal font in the Gothic style with canopied niches enriched with crockets and finials. Another, dating from 1904, stands in nearby College Green with a hexagonal, pyramidal tiled roof and oak screens enclosing a central shaft and drinking bowls, in memory of Samuel Palmer, a local resident (p. 65).

A grand wall fountain in the classical style is inset into the wall of the Theatre Royal, Drury Lane (p. 66). It was financed by public subscription to commemorate the impresario Sir Augustus Harris (1851–96). Two Corinthian pilasters support a pediment crowned by a lyre, forming a canopy over a bronze bust, and the whole stands on a rusticated rough-hewn granite plinth.

Dante Gabriel Rossetti, the Pre-Raphaelite poet-painter, is commemorated by a bronze relief at Chelsea Embankment Gardens, erected through the Association in 1887 (p. 67); as was another to Henry Fawcett, the blind Liberal politician, in Victoria Embankment Gardens, in the same year – the gift of his grateful countrywomen, his wife's family being pioneer suffragettes and feminists, a cause which he literally espoused (p. 67). Nearby stand the sad remains of the Lady Henry Somerset memorial (1897), once crowned by the bronze figure of a girl holding an alms dish by the sculptor George Wade (p. 69). The entire statue was stolen in 1975, but Westminster City Council has arranged for it to be recast in replica from a copy in Portland, Maine.

The drinking-fountain movement was not immune to the contemporary battle of the styles which raged throughout the mid-nineteenth century. Fine examples can be found in a range of Gothic and classical styles, as well as all manner of eclectic combinations. Obelisks, urns and pavilions were common design themes. Many of the plainer memorial fountains are reminiscent of funerary monuments.

The memorial fountain to William Pitt Byrne, former proprietor of the *Morning Post*, in Bryanston Square carries a florid description of the man more suited to a gravestone than a public fountain (p. 70), whilst the nearby obelisk and memorial fountain to Lady Hamilton in Portman Square has a similar sepulchral character (p. 72). Samuel Gurney, the founding father of the Association, is commemorated by a huge granite obelisk fountain at Stratford Broadway in East London.

The most expensive and largest of the ornamental drinking fountains in London was the Victoria Fountain in Victoria Park, donated by Angela Burdett-Coutts (p. 74). It was completed in 1862, at a cost of over £6000, to the designs of Henry Darbishire in a romantic Venetian-Moorish style. The outer pavilion is Moorish, with pointed arches crowned by a cupola complete with clocks and weathervane, but the interior is Renaissance, with huge five-foot putti carrying inverted urns. The bronze cups which were once attached to the fountain were inscribed, 'Temperance is a bridle of gold'. Darbishire also designed the elegant Francis Whiting Memorial Fountain in Guilford Place, Holborn, which carries the familiar figure of the Woman of Samaria (p. 75).

The only rival in opulence to the Burdett-Coutts fountain is the Buxton Memorial fountain in Victoria Tower Gardens, adjoining the Palace of Westminster (p. 76). This Gothic extravaganza, with an enamelled crocketed spire, once stood in Great George Street by Parliament Square, but was moved to its present site in 1957. It resembles a great mediaeval Eleanor cross and was commissioned from S. S. Teulon in 1865 by Charles Buxton MP to commemorate the work of his father and friends in the emancipation of slaves, on the occasion of the triumph of the Union forces in the American Civil War.

The Buxton memorial is typical of the mediaevalism of many fountains. Many, such as those at the old Columbia Market, or at Maidstone in Kent, Settle in Cumbria or Henley in Oxfordshire (p. 77) were designed to resemble mediaeval market crosses, the traditional focus of town and village life throughout England. Hospitals, workhouses and railway stations were also common locations for drinking fountains for the refreshment of weary travellers and those in need. A simple Gothic stone fountain inset into the east wall of St Pancras Station consciously echoes the character of a piscina, but in a secular cathedral of the railway age.

Outside London many local civic authorities followed suit. At Dudley in the West Midlands a huge fountain designed by James Forsyth was donated by the Earl of Dudley in 1867 to stand in the market square (p. 82). It is an exuberant, if somewhat grotesque, affair. It is now dry, but originally water was conducted through two huge dolphins' heads into troughs for horses and through two lions' heads for human consumption. The opening ceremony, covered by the *Illustrated London News*, was a spectacular event with processions of civic dignitaries escorted by the Worcestershire Yeomanry Cavalry.

In the non-conformist strongholds of the north, the temperance movement was particularly strong. One of its doughtiest fighters was Sir Wilfred Lawson (1829–1906) who devoted his life to the cause of abstinence. On his death a splendid memorial drinking fountain and trough were erected at his home town of Aspatria, Cumbria, in 1907 (p. 83). Designed by the sculptor L. Fritz Roselieb, it consists of a sandstone plinth with bronze plaques of Peace and Temperance, over which rises a wonderful Art Nouveau bronze figure of St George slaying the dragon of liquor.

The nearby town of Wigton boasts an equally impressive memorial fountain in the centre of the town (p. 84). It is one of the finest in the country, erected in 1872 by George Moore, High Sheriff of Cumberland, in memory of his wife Eliza.

It was built of hard polished Shap granite and designed by John Knowles with fine bas-relief panels by the famous sculptor Thomas Woolner. Each panel on each face represents Acts of Mercy, over 340 separate castings to Woolner's designs. It is crowned by a spire, with gilded foliated decoration surmounted by a ball and gilded bronze crucifix finial.

Throughout the country there are many examples of fountains which testify to the enthusiasm of local civic reformers. A fine example depicting Rebecca at the well exists outside Bath Abbey, erected in 1861 by the Bath Temperance Society and inscribed 'Water is Best' (p. 85).

However, it was in the north, with its long tradition of radical non-conformism, that many of the most interesting drinking fountains were raised. At Grasmere in the Lake District there is a simple Norman-style drinking fountain, horse and dog trough erected in 1889 as a memorial to William Wordsworth and engraved with a verse from his sonnets (p. 86).

The north-east is particularly well-endowed. In Newcastle a large red stone fountain was erected by the Band of Hope in 1894 near the Cathedral. Later it was moved to the Bigg Market where it resembles a market cross, carrying the same inscription as that in Bath (p. 87). One of the grandest in the city is the W. D. Stephens Memorial Fountain, a fine Edwardian Baroque composition in Clayton Road (p. 88). Stephens, a man of 'open-hearted charity, activity and unfailing geniality', was an ardent supporter of the cause of temperance. At Cullercoats, the Duke of Northumberland gave a site on the sea front for a memorial drinking fountain to Lt. Bryan John Hythwaite Adamson RN, whose ship HMS *Wasp* disappeared without trace off Singapore in 1887. It is a remarkable memorial, with a short Gothic spire and carvings depicting flying wasps (p. 89).

One reason for the popularity of drinking fountains in the area can be traced to the long tradition of 'pants', an old regional word for a fountain. Many villages in the area have simple pants in the form of wells or fountains, which pre-date the drinking-fountain movement. Their importance should not be underestimated. Often they were the sole water supply for the village.

Contrary to common belief, village water supply was often as ill-considered or disorganised as city supply. A simple stone fountain or pant at Long Preston in Cumbria was erected in 1869 by Thomas Holgate to commemorate the work of his father, who first brought water to the village from the neighbouring moor and set up a local gas works on his estate (p. 91). The water system is still run as a charitable trust. In the remote village of Dent in Yorkshire the sole source of water until the 1920s was a memorial fountain built to commemorate its most famous son, Adam Sedgwick, Professor of Geology at Cambridge University (p. 92).

Usually village fountains were simple unadorned structures, but occasionally a more flamboyant approach was adopted. The availability of a wide range of cast-iron designs from the great iron foundries enabled patrons to select designs from standard catalogues.

Two splendid examples survive at Middleton-in-Teesdale, County
Durham (p. 93), and at Nenthead, Cumbria (p. 93) both to the same
design – an elaborate cast-iron canopy with engrailed arches over a
central pump. The former, with a boy and dolphin centrepiece,
painted to accentuate its detailing, has playful crocodiles on the
inside spandrels of the arches. They were erected by R. W.
Bainbridge of Middleton House, whose local lead company had
extensive mining operations in the area.

An even more exotic extravaganza can be found at Shildon in
County Durham, where the ornate cast-iron canopy is enriched
with embossed plaques depicting the 'Royal George', an early
railway engine built in the local engineering works. Other cast-iron
canopies from pattern books can be traced from as far apart as
Mowbray Park in Sunderland to the Princess Gardens, Cowes, Isle
of Wight, the latter having been restored recently with the aid of a
grant from the Association.

Whilst iron was common for both free-standing and wall
fountains, tiled or ceramic fountains were, surprisingly, relatively
unusual. A notable exception using Doulton ceramics enriched with
sinuous Art Nouveau details stands in Alexandra Road, Clevedon.

The importance of a reliable source of fresh water for remote
village communities cannot be overstated. It had a profound effect
on the religious, social and cultural development of many regions of
Britain, and this was reflected in ancient local folklore and
traditions.

In Derbyshire, for instance, a unique and unusual tradition
developed of well-dressing. Today this mysterious custom is
preserved almost exclusively in this county. Tissington is the oldest
and most interesting survival. It is of pre-Roman, or pagan origin,
but in recent years it has undergone a great resurgence.

Once well-worship prevailed in every part of England and it is
easy to see why. As a perpetually renewing source of life, water was
endowed with supernatural qualities. In some areas the water
possessed medicinal value and was renowned for healing certain

complaints, particularly eye troubles; and in an age when ophthalmic complaints were rife, this probably had a firm foundation in fact. Distant pagan beliefs in nature worship were reinforced by the Romans and later by Christianity. The Roman sage Seneca averred that 'Where a spring rises or a river flows, there ought we to build altars and offer sacrifices.'

Later the Saxon king Edgar, and the Dane Canute (1018) issued edicts prohibiting the worship of wells and fountains. In the canons of Anselm of 1102 we find a compromise in the order that 'no one shall attribute sanctity to a fountain without the bishop's authority.'

In the west and north of England countless legends and country rhymes attest to the power of local superstition. The red stain of iron on chalybeate springs was often mistaken for blood, fostering a whole range of wild local tales. In the north many sources of water are supposed to be inhabited by local deities. For instance, the river Tees is associated with the sinister Peg Powler.

Well-dressing probably originated in pagan sacrifices to water-gods as a thanksgiving for past supplies and as a plea for further favour. The Romans celebrated the festival of Fontanalia on the Ides of October in honour of the nymphs of wells and fountains. Later the practice was absorbed by the Christian Church. Today well-dressing in Derbyshire has strong religious themes and is carried out at various dates between May and August.

As the social centre of village life, wells were often used for baptisms, but over generations, like many holy wells, they degenerated into 'wishing wells', pale reflections of their ancient pagan origins. In Cornwall the throwing in of pins was a common custom at wishing wells. At Ragwell near Newcastle rags were presented as votive offerings.

The popularity of spas arose directly from pre-Christian traditions of pagan wells and from later Christian holy wells. The development of spas is a subject which lies outside the scope of this small book, but both Buxton and Bath had springs that were used by the Romans for health and relaxation. By the eighteenth century there were literally hundreds of spas ranging in size from Cheltenham, Harrogate and Tunbridge Wells through smaller resorts, such as Epsom, Malvern and Leamington, to suburbs around London, such as Sadler's Wells, Bagnigge Wells and Marylebone gardens.

The London spas were mostly pretty small affairs. As early as the eleventh century Muswell Hill was known for the curative properties of its waters. In 1112 a chapel known as Our Lady of Muswell was built over it. Much later, in 1698, Hampstead enjoyed a national reputation from its development of a chalybeate or ferruginous spring at Well Walk.

The prophylactic benefits of taking the waters were eulogised in a poem published in 1655 and entitled 'To a Friend upon a Journey to Epsom Well':

Some drink of it, and in an houre,
Their Stomach, Guts and Kidneys scower;
Others doe Bathe, and ulcers cure,
Dry Itch, and Leprosie impure;
And what in Lords you call the Gout,
In poor the Pox, this drives all out.

Throughout the nineteenth century the problem of village water supply exercised many communities, but at Stoke Row in the Chilterns it was solved by an extraordinary piece of munificence. A local resident, Edward Anderton Reade, the fifth son of the Squire of Ipsden, served a long and distinguished career in India for over thirty-four years, culminating in his appointment as Lieutenant-Governor of the North-West Provinces. In his long career he built up a close relationship with the Maharajah of Benares, aiding him through the difficult years of the Indian Mutiny. On Reade's retirement to England, the Maharajah wanted to mark his service by a donation to a charity and, recalling how Reade compared the water problems of Benares to his own native Chilterns, he donated funds for a well in his village. The cast-iron well, crowned by a gilt elephant and surmounted by a splendid Mughal dome, was completed in May 1864 and opened on Queen Victoria's birthday (p. 95). It is a remarkable structure of considerable interest, and a notable feat of engineering, the well shaft being over 368 feet deep.

This benefaction provoked widespread comment in both Britain and India and prompted others to follow suit. Not to be outdone by his countryman, with the aid of the Association, in 1868 the Maharajah of Vizianagram erected a huge Gothic memorial fountain in Hyde Park to the designs of Robert Keirle. Somewhat ungratefully, the memorial was demolished for road widening in the early 1960s.

Another Indian donation, which does survive, can be found in Broad Walk, Regent's Park, where the aptly-named Parsee benefactor, Sir Cowasjee Jehangheer Readymoney, donated £1400 in 1869 to mark the protection enjoyed by him and his fellow Parsees under British rule in India (p. 96). It was vilified by *The Standard*, which remarked in 1869 that 'It is however, not confined to any special style of architecture, and it would be difficult to say what ideas of taste have been adhered to, or which canons have been most violated in the design.'

These generous Imperial benefactions were more than compensated for by the activity of the Association overseas. As its reputation grew, requests for assistance and advice came in from all over the world. As early as 1864 a fine Gothic drinking-fountain designed by J. F. Bentley, with allegorical panels of bas-relief by Thomas Earp, was sent to Bridgetown, Barbados. Later drinking-fountains and cattle troughs were erected as far afield as Japan, Korea, Syria, India, Rumania, France and Palestine.

In 1878 Paris boasted fifty-six fountains, fifty of which were directly due to the generosity of Sir Richard Wallace, the famous Anglo-Parisian philanthropist, who at his own cost erected fountains similar to those in London throughout the French capital. To recall his largesse a typical French cast-iron drinking fountain with caryatids stands in the forecourt of the Wallace Collection in

Manchester Square, London (p. 99). Another identical example can be found in New Orleans.

Although the Imperial dimension was never very great, royalty played an increasingly important role. In 1877 Queen Victoria had donated a fountain and trough through the Association to the village of Esher, but the Golden Jubilee of 1887, and the Diamond Jubilee ten years later, provoked an enormous wave of interest in commemorative civic memorials including drinking fountains.

In London a notable fountain was erected in New Oxford Street by the Board of Works for the St Giles District to mark the Diamond Jubilee (p. 102). Built of polished red granite, it was designed in a ponderous Romanesque style, enriched with carved and etched foliated ornament. At Jedburgh the Golden Jubilee Memorial with bas reliefs of the Queen was sited at the central crossroads to resemble a market cross, whilst in Hexham the Temperley Memorial Fountain was raised 'for the common good' in Renaissance style to replace an earlier stone pant (p. 103). It carries an effusive inscription by a local poet, Wilson Gibson, which begins:

> O you who drink my cooling waters clear
> Forget not the far hills from whence they flow . . .
> Wherever fen and moorland, year by year,
> Spring, summer, autumn, winter, come and go.

More typical were the simple stone memorials raised in countless villages and towns throughout the country. At Slaidburn is a typical Jubilee village fountain in a robust style entirely appropriate to the bluff character of the Lancashire village where it stands (p. 104). Sedbergh has a lovely Diamond Jubilee drinking-fountain set into the churchyard wall with a segmental pediment depicting the Woman of Samaria and Our Saviour at the well, now protected under glass (p. 105). Not far from the Maharajah's well at Stoke Row, the village of Lee has a pretty Arts and Crafts Jubilee well beneath a picturesque tiled roof.

Although the royal perspective reached its apogee under Victoria, it did not wane immediately. In 1911 the Jewish community of the East End raised a splendid memorial fountain in the Whitechapel Road in memory of King Edward VII (pp. 106–7). Designed by W. S. Frith, it is crowned by the figure of a winged angel and comprises a stone obelisk flanked by bronze figures of Justice and Liberty, the latter holding a 1911 motor car and steamship, symbols of scientific progress.

A year earlier a magnificent memorial drinking fountain had been completed on the summit of Colley Hill outside Reigate, the gift of Colonel Robert Inglis as a memorial to Captain George Simpson. It was designed by the architects Seth-Smith and Monro as an hexagonal classical pavilion with a shallow saucer dome embellished with mosaic work depicting the exact positions of the planets on 1 December 1909. According to a contemporary newspaper account, it was hoped that 'the young men and maidens of Reigate can refresh themselves after their toil in climbing up from the town, preparatory to exchanging their sweet confidences, as in old classical times.'

Considering the vast number of First and Second World War memorials which were raised, surprisingly few were designed as drinking fountains. At Langcliffe, North Yorkshire, the village losses are recorded on a poignant stone fountain crowned by a simple cross (p. 108). The Boer War produced a fine pair of examples in Northumberland. At Bellingham the figure of a soldier with rifle reversed stands under a weatherbeaten stone canopy (p. 109). At nearby Allendale another recalls John Joseph Glendinning of the Imperial Yeomanry who was killed at Klip Drift, South Africa on 7 March 1902.

The Association ceased to erect granite troughs after 1936 on the grounds of expense and because modes of transport were changing. However the trend towards motor traffic was not straightforward. In the 1930s the use of horse-drawn vehicles actually increased, as there was a distinct revival of their use for domestic deliveries of milk and groceries in the expanding city suburbs. Gradually the Association concentrated more and more on the provision of drinking fountains in schools and public gardens. In the same year a programme was commenced to replace insanitary cups and chains by modern upward jets of water. The temperance movement remained a potent force. As late as 1935 the British Women's Total Abstinence Union erected a drinking-fountain at Manor Park, Sutton, surmounted by a stylised stone figure of a child. In 1929 a new utility model for fountains was introduced which is still commonly found in parks and public spaces throughout the country. It is a simple pillar design made initially of granolithic and later of terrazzo with an upward bubble jet from a bronze surround. In 1945 the Royal Society of Arts organised a national competition for a superior design which would be suitable for more sensitive locations such as Royal Parks. Unfortunately none of the 192 entries was deemed successful, and in 1950 the Association commissioned Lutyens and Greenwood to design a metal fountain. Although not entirely satisfactory, seven were produced for the Royal Parks.

Six years later Stephen Dykes Bower designed an alternative in aluminium alloy with a parabolic jet. Three were presented to Kew Gardens in 1956. In 1955 the same architect designed the Coronation drinking fountain at the Palace of Westminster to commemorate the accession of Queen Elizabeth II. In recent months Westminster City Council has commissioned an elegant new stone fountain for use within the city to replace many of the old vandalised granolithic models.

The Association is still very active, providing new facilities in schools and playgrounds across the country and encouraging the restoration of existing fountains. New castings of the original bronze lion's-head spouts have been made. In 1986 an old granite horse trough was relocated from Blackfriars to Hyde Park to commemorate the horses killed in the IRA terrorist bombing of the Household Cavalry two years earlier. A new Peter Pan drinking fountain by the sculptress Catherine Moor Johnson was unveiled at the Hospital for Sick Children in Great Ormond Street in May 1988, whilst work is in hand on a bronze replica of the Wills fountain from Blackfriars Bridge for use at Wolfson College, Cambridge.

Today it is difficult to grasp that the horse troughs erected by the Association were the filling stations of their day, or that the quaint items of street furniture, which drinking fountains have now become, provided a basic necessity of life which saved thousands of lives from inebriety and disease. With the advent of motor transport and with purified drinking water piped to every home in the land as a right rather than a benefit, the principal social function of the Association has long been superseded, but the monuments which survive bear witness to ideals and attitudes long since forgotten. As such they illuminate areas of the Victorian mind and moral preoccupations which are completely alien to us today. Accordingly their social significance is as important a reason for preserving those that survive as the architectural contribution which they make to the character and appearance of city streets and village greens. Many are now listed as historic buildings and afforded statutory protection from unauthorised alteration or removal, but very few are in working order and most are shamefully neglected.

The case for the proper conservation of these fascinating items of street furniture is a compelling one, but unless it is heeded urgently by local authorities and councils throughout the country, a significant aspect of the national heritage will have been lost forever.

ISLINGTON GREEN: 1862. No less a person than Gladstone unveiled the memorial statue and drinking fountain to Sir Hugh Myddleton, mastermind and builder of the New River, which transformed the water supply to seventeenth-century London. The monument, raised by public subscription, was designed in marble by John Thomas, with a full-size figure of Myddleton flanked by two cherubs, from whose jars water cascaded in to the bowls beneath.

facing page BEDFORD ROW, HOLBORN: early nineteenth-century.
Pumps such as these were once the principal source of water for
thousands of people.

above ST. SEPULCHRE'S CHURCH, SNOW HILL: 1859. The
surviving central portion of the first drinking fountain erected by
the Metropolitan Free Drinking Fountain Association. Presented by
the founder Samuel Gurney MP, it was opened amid scenes of public
rejoicing and was soon used by over 7000 people every day. The
fountain still retains its original bronze cups and chains.

WEST SMITHFIELD GARDEN: 1871. This lovely figure of Peace,
crowned by a wheaten garland, and designed by the sculptor
J. Birnie Philip, was the centrepiece of a much larger drinking
fountain erected by the City Corporation using the accumulated
interest on a mediaeval legacy bequeathed by Sir Martin Bowes, a
former Lord Mayor. Designed by Francis Butler, originally it
comprised a huge stone canopy in an eclectic style with four corner
figures representing Temperance, Faith, Hope and Charity.
Unfortunately the superstructure fell into disrepair and was taken
down, leaving only the base and central statue.

ROSSLYN HILL, HAMPSTEAD: *c* 1875. Evangelism and water often flowed hand in hand, as this florid wall fountain conveys.

ALLITSEN ROAD, ST. JOHN'S WOOD: 1861. This early Association
wall fountain carries the words of Christ in tablets of stone.

RICHMOND HILL: 1891. Winged dragons, flamboyant ironwork
and octagonal lanterns commemorate the Royal Society for the
Prevention of Cruelty to Animals on this iron arbour designed by
the eminent architect T. E. Collcutt. Ornamental marigolds have
replaced the basins of water beneath.

facing page, top   DOUBLE HORSE TROUGH, ALBANY STREET: *c* 1875. A typical Association double trough, still in use today.

facing page, bottom   HIGH ROAD, WOOD GREEN: This Association cattle trough outside the Fishmonger's Arms public house verges on the Baroque with its scrolled centrepiece and boar's head. Cattle were driven on the hoof past here to the London markets.

above   TOOLEY STREET, SOUTHWARK: *c* 1930. You can lead a horse to water, but you cannot force it to drink. Few needed any encouragement to use Association troughs at a time when horses and cattle were cruelly abused. This pair are enjoying two singles and a double. Horse-drawn traffic was commonplace until the 1950s.

above left   ROYAL EXCHANGE: 1878. Mediaeval guilds played an important role in supplying water to the City and they continued their philanthropic support in to the late nineteenth century. This beautiful sculpture by Jules Dalou was designed by the architect J. Edmeston and presented by John Whittaker Ellis, with assistance from the Draper's and Merchant Taylors' companies.

above right, and detail on facing page   ROYAL EXCHANGE: 1911. This Ionic canopy sheltering a chaste bronze nude was erected to mark the Golden Jubilee of the Association in 1909. It was designed by Josiah Gunton and unveiled by the Lord Mayor. Each face of the plinth carries a bronze plaque commemorating the Association.

above right BLACKFRIARS BRIDGE: 1861. This delightful
drinking-fountain, presented by Samuel Gurney, was placed by the
Association beside the Royal Exchange in 1861, and later moved to
its present site in 1911. It is of particular importance as it was one of
the first to use the symbolic figure of Temperance on a public
drinking-fountain, and it still bears a bronze plaque carrying the
original name of the Association. The figure, designed by Wills
Bros., was cast by the Coalbrookdale Iron Company.

CLAPHAM COMMON: 1884. Charles Barry, architect of the Houses of Parliament, designed this magnificent memorial which once stood in Adelaide Place in the City of London; but it proved too heavy for the vaults beneath and was moved to its present position in 1895. It was raised by the United Kingdom Temperance and General Provident Institution, whose plaque it bears. The figures were sculpted by A. von Kréling, a German sculptor, and cast in Munich. They depict the Woman of Samaria offering sustenance to a thirsty cripple. Unfortunately the fine lions masks no longer spout water, but the later taps still work.

GLOUCESTER GATE, REGENT'S PARK: 1878. Echoes of Elysium.
This bewitching memorial drinking fountain conjures with all the
romantic imagery of an idealised pastoral scene. It was presented by
Matilda, the wife of Richard Kent Jr., a local churchwarden and
comprises a bronze statue of a milkmaid with her pail astride a
barren rocky slope. The sculptor was Joseph Durham. Neglected by
Camden Council for many years, it has finally been restored.

PIMLICO ROAD: 1871. This elegant Italianate memorial drinking fountain was presented via the Association in memory of the Second Marquess of Westminster by his family. The shell-capped niches are embellished with rich panels of polychrome mosaic.

ST. GEORGE'S HOSPITAL, HYDE PARK CORNER: 1860. Hospitals, like churches, were seen as appropriate locations for drinking fountains, providing life-saving, free fresh water for those in need. This early example, erected by the Association and enriched with a shell bowl and scrolled ornament, evokes the popular imagery of an idyllic classical spring providing succour for the poor.

THE GREEK BOY FOUNTAIN, ST. JAMES'S PARK: 1863. Designed by
C. H. Mabey, this delightful ornamental drinking fountain was
erected by the Association for H. M. Office of Works in 1863. The
marble scallop shell water bowls, to designs by R. Jackson, were
added two years later. They are enriched with dolphins' heads and
carved foliated decoration. The figure, which was smashed by
vandals in 1988, is now being restored.

OLD ST. PANCRAS CHURCHYARD: 1877. This eloquent example of prefabricated cast-iron work was manufactured by Andrew Handyside & Co. of Derby to a classical design based on the Choragic monument of Lysicrates in Athens. Still in its original dark green livery, it was donated by William Thornton, a senior churchwarden, and is one of the most refined surviving examples of a cast-iron drinking fountain in the country.

KEW GARDENS ENTRANCE SCREEN: 1863. This jaunty little marble
cherub carries a sash engraved with the words 'Good Health',
carefully draped to protect the parts that the water will eventually
reach. It was designed by John Bell and installed in an outer niche
of the main entrance screen to the gardens by H. M. Office of
Works in 1863. The basin was added by the Association a year later.

ALBERT GARDENS, STEPNEY: 1903. This cast-iron shepherd boy in classical attire and complete with rake, sickle and wheatsheaf was cast in a French foundry, the Fonderie D'Art.

HAMPSTEAD HEATH EXTENSION: 1907. Ambrosia for the Gods. This Baroque vase set among the trees of Hampstead Heath was presented by Emily Field, a leading light of the Hampstead Heath Preservation Society in memory of her husband, the artist, Walter Field.

KENSINGTON GARDENS, MARLBOROUGH GATE: 1939. Wrestling
bears. This playful little drinking fountain was designed by the
sculptor K. Keeble Smith just before the outbreak of the Second
World War to mark the eightieth anniversary of the Association.

LINCOLN'S INN FIELDS, HOLBORN: 1882. This grand two-storey drinking fountain in Italianate style was erected as a token of love and esteem by Mrs Twells in memory of her husband, Philip Twells, the local MP.

LINCOLN'S INN FIELDS: NORTH-WEST CORNER: 1861. This
splendid gabled Gothic memorial, presented by Mr Martin Ware
through the Association, had a distinct Celtic character now
diminished by the loss of its original stone cross finial. It is
inscribed with the same quotation as that at St Dunstan's – 'The
Fear of the Lord is a Fountain of Life'. Sadly neglected, this
important listed monument is in urgent need of restoration.

ST. DUNSTAN'S-IN-THE-WEST CHURCH, FLEET STREET: 1860.
Inscribed 'The Fear of the Lord is a Fountain of Life', this elaborate
wall fountain with a dolphin's head spout was installed in the
church railings as the gift of Sir James Duke MP. By siting fountains
in such locations, philanthropists reinforced the importance of the
church in the local community. Water was not merely an essential
for life, but a symbol of spiritual purity and moral cleansing.

SOUTH END GREEN, HAMPSTEAD: 1881. This great Gothic
monument was designed by J. H. Evins for Miss Crump of
Hereford House, in memory of William Warburton Pearce and of
her uncle J. B. Chamberlain, who died the previous year. It
epitomises Victorian ideals of civic design.

COLLEGE GREEN, HAMPSTEAD: 1904. Resembling a rather elegant gazebo, this Association fountain was presented in memory of Samuel Palmer of North Court, Hampstead by his widow and family. Designed in a mixture of Gothic and Arts and Crafts styles, the sides are enclosed by ornamental oak screens.

THEATRE ROYAL, DRURY LANE: SIR AUGUSTUS HARRIS
MEMORIAL DRINKING FOUNTAIN: 1897. Sir Augustus Harris
(1851–96) was a popular impressario who 'resuscitated the Drury
Lane Theatre when it had fallen on evil times'. On his death this
magnificent memorial, designed by Sidney R. J. Smith, was raised by
public subscription. It boasts a bronze bust of Harris by Sir Thomas
Brock set in a pedimented bay flanked by Corinthian columns, each
enriched with bronze reliefs of musical trophies. Playful
Renaissance cherubs cavort over the rough-hewn granite base.

above left CHELSEA EMBANKMENT GARDENS: 1887 In his later years Dante Gabriel Rossetti (1828–82) lived at No 16 Cheyne Walk. On his death a fine memorial drinking fountain was built in the nearby Embankment Gardens. Designed by the architect J. P. Seddon, the bronze bust was the work of his friend and follower Ford Madox Brown. On the reverse of the monument is a plaque with a list of subscribers including Millais, Alma-Tadema, Lord Leighton, and Holman Hunt.

above right VICTORIA EMBANKMENT GARDENS, TEMPLE: 1887. Although blind from a shooting accident when young, Henry Fawcett (1833–84) was a remarkable Liberal politician who is commemorated by a bronze medallion, the centrepiece of a memorial drinking fountain, erected by his grateful countrywomen. The bronze, designed by Mary Grant, carries a graphic portrayal of his blindness. The overall design was the work of Basil Champneys.

CHEYNE WALK, CHELSEA: 1880. This grey granite drinking
fountain combined with four corner horse troughs was designed by
the architect Charles Barry. It was one of a number erected as
commemorative memorials. The Webster Memorial fountain in
Dulwich is to the same design. This example at Chelsea recalls the
late George Sparkes of Bromley, former judge at Madras, 'a great
and good man gifted with every refined feeling and much esteemed
by all who knew him'.

VICTORIA EMBANKMENT GARDENS: 1897. 'I was thirsty and ye gave me drink.' Erected in memory of Lady Henry Somerset by the Children of the Loyal Temperance League, this touching little memorial, stolen in 1971, is to be recast in replica. The bronze figure of a small girl standing on a cairn of stones and holding out an alms dish was designed by George Wade in 1897.

facing page BRYANSTON SQUARE, MARYLEBONE: THE WILLIAM
PITT BYRNE MEMORIAL FOUNTAIN: 1862. This elegant memorial
recalls the funerary monuments of antiquity. Erected on a cairn of
red and yellow Mansfield stone, the upper part is of white marble
and carries a tablet of green serpentine bearing arms and a florid
inscription. It records the 'unobtrusive piety and practical charity'
of the former editor of the *Morning Post* and closes the vista from
Great Cumberland Place where he once lived.

above ST. MARTIN'S-IN-THE-FIELDS CHURCHYARD: 1886.
Resembling a tomb and standing in a forgotten corner of the
churchyard, this fine marble drinking fountain marks the life of
John Law Baker of the Madras Army. Note the wonderful lions
heads on the base of the plinth to the crowning fluted column. Alas,
the bowls have been sealed with concrete.

PORTMAN SQUARE, MARYLEBONE: 1878. Reminiscent of a funerary monument, this memorial drinking fountain was raised by Lady Hamilton, the widow of Sir James Hamilton. It was Lady Hamilton who designed the acorn jets found on many fountains of the period after public comments were made about the unseemliness of water flowing from the mouths of animals. Constructed of polished red granite, the fountain is inscribed: 'Jesus cried if any man thirst, let him come unto me and drink'. A small bronze plaque carries a further Biblical inscription.

OLD STREET, SHOREDITCH: 1880. This regal-looking column and crowning orb was raised by the vestry of St Leonard's, Shoreditch.

VICTORIA PARK, HACKNEY: THE VICTORIA FOUNTAIN: 1862.
Built to the designs of the architect Henry Darbishire in a Venetian-
Moorish style, the Victoria Fountain was one of the grandest
drinking fountains erected in Britain and cost nearly £6000. It was
presented through the Association by the heiress Angela Burdett-
Coutts and carries the inscription 'For the Love of God and
Country, the Victoria Fountain given anno domini 1862'. Crowned
by a green slate cupola embellished with clocks, it offered fresh
drinking water as the centrepiece of a new 200-acre park providing
open air for the East End poor. Over 10,000 people attended the
opening.

GUILFORD PLACE, HOLBORN: 1870. The Francis Whiting Memorial Fountain, opposite the site of the old Foundling Hospital, was designed by the architect Henry Darbishire and presented by the Misses Whiting to commemorate their mother. The cylindrical smooth granite drum on a rough-hewn granite base is crowned by a captivating figure of the Woman of Samaria.

VICTORIA TOWER GARDENS: 1865. Romantic mediaevalism run riot. This remarkable High Victorian Gothic monument has a spire enriched with brightly-coloured enamelled iron plates. Presented by Charles Buxton MP, a stalwart of the Association, in collaboration with the architect S. S. Teulon, it originally stood in Great George Street by Parliament Square before it was removed to its present site in 1957. It commemorates the work of his father, Sir Thomas Fowell Buxton, and those associated with him in the great emancipation of slaves throughout the British Empire in 1834, and it was raised to celebrate the final extinction of slavery with the victory of the Union forces in the American Civil War.

HENLEY-ON-THAMES, OXFORDSHIRE: 1885.

'O ye fountains bless ye the Lord
Praise and exalt Him above all for ever.'

This great crocketted and pinnacled Gothic cross was raised in
memory of Greville Phillimore, rector of the town, by his family
and friends to mark sixteen years of civic service. It was designed by
James Forsyth and consciously resembles the great market crosses
of the Middle Ages. Note the multi-lobed steps and dog trough at
the base.

STREATHAM GREEN: 1862. High Victorian Gothic. This polychrome Gothic gable is inscribed with the words 'For I Will Pour Water Upon Him That Is Thirsty'. It was given and probably designed by the local painter William Dyce, benefactor of nearby St Leonard's church.

BAYSWATER ROAD: 1872. A typical wall fountain taken from the
Association's catalogue.

above left FINSBURY SQUARE: 1899. This elaborate example of
late-Victorian eclecticism, enriched with grotesque masks and
dolphins, was presented to the Parish of St Luke by Thomas and
Walter Smith in memory of their mother, Martha Smith. Adjacent
are two granite troughs, one to her memory and the other to that of
the Queen. The date of birth of Martha Smith varies on both
monuments – 1825 on one and 1826 on the other.

above right ROEHAMPTON LANE, PUTNEY: 1882. This austere
Doric kiosk in grey and red granite stands on an island site flanked
by cambered-shaped horse troughs. It was designed by
J. C. Radford for Mrs Lyne Stephens. At the centre is a beguiling
bronze fountain group by Henry Dasson portraying putti and fish.
The reverse still retains an original dolphin gargoyle spout.

HANS PLACE, KNIGHTSBRIDGE: *c* 1886. 'No braver soldier or more brilliant leader of men ever wore the Queen's uniform.' Major-General Sir Herbert Stewart was considered by Lord Wolseley and others to be one of the most gifted officers of his generation. He was mortally wounded at Abu Klea in the advance to relieve General Gordon in Khartoum in January 1885. The broken granite obelisk symbolises a life cut short in its prime. At the base is a small bronze depicting Stewart and a later inscription to his son.

DUDLEY, WEST MIDLANDS: 1867. This spectacular fountain, shown here in its original state, was probably the grandest to be erected outside London. It was designed by James Forsyth and presented to the town by the Earl of Dudley, where it stands in the Market Square. Like a number of Forsyth's wilder compositions, it makes up in sheer ebullience for what it lacks in artistic discipline.

ASPATRIA, CUMBRIA: 1907. St George slaying the Dragon of
Liquor. This magnificent memorial to Sir William Lawson (1829–
1906), one of the most resolute supporters of the Temperance cause,
was designed by the sculptor L. Fritz Roselieb in a wonderful Art
Nouveau style. Sinuous bronze bowls adorned with stylised
dolphins once received water from the masks above. The plinth is
graced with panels of bronze relief of Lawson and the spirits of
Peace and Temperance. At the front is a plain granite horse trough.

WIGTON: CUMBRIA: THE MOORE MEMORIAL DRINKING
FOUNTAIN, 1872–3. Designed by J. T. Knowles in polished Shap
granite, the Moore Memorial was one of the finest drinking-
fountains ever erected. Built by a local philanthropist and Sheriff of
Cumberland to commemorate his wife, Eliza, it dominates the
centre of the town. Each face carries aluminium bronze panels
depicting Acts of Mercy by the eminent sculptor Thomas Woolner.
Above are pediments enclosing medallion busts of Mrs Moore and
an elaborately carved pyramidal spire with gilded foliated
decoration, crowned by an orb and cross gilt bronze finial. It cost
over £12,000.

BATH: 1861. Water is Best. The Temperance message portrayed graphically in stone outside the portals of Bath Abbey using the family Biblical symbol of Rebecca at the Well.

GRASMERE, CUMBRIA: 1889.

   'Blessings be with them and eternal praise
   Who gave us nobler loves and nobler cares'

The Wordsworth memorial drinking fountain and cattle trough.
Situated a few hundred yards from his home in the Lake District
and resembling some mediaeval roadside shrine, this simple but
effective Norman-style monument is a most eloquent and
unexpected reminder of the great man.

BIGG MARKET, NEWCASTLE-UPON-TYNE: 1894. Originally erected near the Cathedral, this large red sandstone fountain was later moved to the Bigg Market where it resembles a market cross. It was raised by the Band of Hope Union in a mixture of Jacobean and Renaissance styles and commemorates J. H. Rutherford. It is inscribed with the Temperance message 'Water is Best' and was presented by Joseph Cowan.

NEWCASTLE-UPON-TYNE: CLAYTON ROAD: THE W. D. STEPHENS
MEMORIAL DRINKING FOUNTAIN 1901. Designed by Marshall and
Tweedy in Edwardian civic classical style and paid for by public
subscription, the pedimented centrepiece is flanked by obelisks
enriched with garlands, swags and ornamental railings. The bronze
roundel by W. Donaldson depicts Stephens (1827–1901), former
Sheriff and Mayor and 'A citizen of Lofty Ideals and Strenuous
Endeavour', to mark his association with the Temperance
movement.

CULLERCOATS, TYNE AND WEAR: 1886. This unusual monument
with its fluted spire recalls the strange death of Lt. Bryan John
Huthwaite Adamson whose ship, H.M.S. *Wasp*, disappeared without
trace off Singapore in September 1887.

ICKENHAM, MIDDLESEX: 1866. This picturesque octagonal tiled pavilion with its twisted barley-sugar columns covers a cast-iron Gothic well and pump, which was erected by the executors of the late Charlotte Gell, a local resident who died in 1863. Pumps like these were often the principal water supply for many towns and villages all over Britain until the advent of piped water supplies well into the early twentieth century.

PRESENTED
BY
THOMAS HOLGATE
OF BROOKLANDS
IN MEMORY OF
HIS FATHER
A.D. 1869

LONG PRESTON: 1869. Typical of many simple stone pants that were erected in the north of England, this one was raised by Thomas Holgate to mark the work of his father who first brought water to the village.

DENT, WEST YORKSHIRE: THE ADAM SEDGWICK MEMORIAL
DRINKING FOUNTAIN. The supply of fresh water to remote rural
towns and villages was a persistent problem well into the twentieth
century. Sedgwick (1785–1873) was a pioneer geologist who was
born in Dent and later became Professor of Geology at Trinity
College, Cambridge. His memorial drinking fountain, hewn from a
huge block of local stone and opened shortly after his death, was
the sole source of water for the entire village until the 1920s.

above left MIDDLETON-IN-TEESDALE, CO. DURHAM: 1879. One of a pair with that at Nenthead, this example is more cherished and has been highlighted in black, red and yellow. Note the playful crocodiles to the spandrels. It is typical of many of the designs available from the standard ironwork catalogues of the period. This was cast by Glenfield and Kennedy of Kilmarnock.

above right NENTHEAD, CUMBRIA: 1879. This ornate cast-iron canopy enriched with engrailed arches covers a simple pump. It was erected by R. W. Bainbridge of Middleton House 'in commemoration of a testimonial presented to him and Mrs Bainbridge by the employees of the London Lead Company and other friends'.

BUXTON, DERBYSHIRE: 1940. 'A Well of Living Waters'. This simple but touching memorial well stands on the site of a much older pump, St Ann's Well, and was dedicated to Emilie Dorothy Bounds, a local councillor, by her husband and daughter. The central mosaic niche shelters a bronze group of the Virgin and Female Child. Buxton was renowned for its waters as early as Roman times.

STOKE ROW, OXFORDSHIRE: 1864. The Maharajah's well. This exotic vision of India in the Chiltern Hills was the result of the close relationship between the Maharajah of Benares and a local resident, Edward Anderton Reade, who served there for over 34 years. Examination reveals the details to be European rather than Indian. It was designed by Reade and built by the Wallingford firm of R. J. & H. Wilder.

BROAD WALK, REGENT'S PARK: 1869. Known as the Parsee
fountain after its benefactor, Sir Cowasjee Jehangheer Readymoney,
the monument was presented as a token of gratitude to the people
of England for the protection enjoyed by him and his Parsee fellow-
countrymen under British rule in India. It was designed by the
Association's own architect, Robert Keirle, at a cost of £1400 and
boasts ten tons of Sicilian marble and four tons of Aberdeen granite.
On three faces are carved busts depicting the donor, the Prince
Consort and the Queen; the fourth once carried a clock. When it
was opened by Princess Mary, Duchess of Teck, *Punch* could not
resist sending up Mr Readymoney's 'Parsee-money'.

KIRKBY LONSDALE, CUMBRIA: 1868. This impressive wall fountain and trough set in a wide low Norman arch at the edge of the churchyard was erected to commemorate the restoration of the parish church by Lord Kenlis, whose arms are emblazoned above.

RICHMOND PARK: 1887. Typical of many wall fountains, this chaste example at Richmond Park has a small plate indicating that it is equipped with Maignen's Patent Filtre-Rapide to protect the user from too much calcium.

HERTFORD HOUSE, MANCHESTER SQUARE, MARYLEBONE. *c* 1878.
One of a hundred drinking fountains presented to Paris by Sir
Richard Wallace and designed by Charles Lebourg. Four caryatids
carry a canopy embellished with simulated fish-scale details. The
plinth is enriched with scrolled consoles and moulded dolphins.
This example was presented to the Wallace Collection by
Shoreditch Borough Council in 1959.

BERKELEY SQUARE, MAYFAIR: 1881. Pre-Raphaelite variations on
the theme of Temperance. Erected by the Association in the heart of
the fashionable West End of London, this accomplished rendition
of the Woman of Samaria was the work of the Pre-Raphaelite
sculptor Alexander Monro. The fountain was the gift of Henry,
third Marquess of Lansdowne.

ST. GEORGE'S, HANOVER SQUARE GARDENS, MOUNT STREET, MAYFAIR: 1892. This elegant equestrian bronze with lion masks at the base was erected by Henry Lofts in recognition of many happy years in Mount Street. It was designed by Sir Ernest George and is still in working order.

NEW OXFORD STREET, HOLBORN: 1897. This rather ponderous pile of polished granite is typical of many memorial drinking fountains erected to mark Queen Victoria's two Jubilees. It was presented by the Association for the St Giles's Board of Works and is an interesting piece of street furniture. Until recently its setting was enhanced by a pair of K2 telephone kiosks, designed by Giles Gilbert Scott, but to their everlasting shame, these were replaced in 1987 with discordant new steel booths by British Telecom.

HEXHAM, NORTHUMBERLAND: 1901. The Temperley Memorial fountain is an elaborate column in Renaissance style raised to mark the last year of the reign of Queen Victoria and the first of Edward VII. Marked by the passage of time, today it could easily be mistaken for a mediaeval market cross.

SLAIDBURN: 1887. This robust stone Golden Jubilee memorial
fountain provided an important public facility for the entire village.

SEDBERGH: 1897. This Diamond Jubilee memorial fountain is typical of many with its Biblical allusions and prominent location on the churchyard wall.

WHITECHAPEL ROAD: 1911. Jewish munificence. The Jews of the East End of London had a long tradition of philanthropic works. This superb monument by W. S. Frith was raised by the Jewish community to commemorate Edward VII. Crowned by a winged angel and flanked by statues of Liberty and Justice, it is one of the finest London memorials of the period. Its dilapidated condition is a standing reproach to those entrusted with its care and maintenance.

LANGCLIFFE, NORTH YORKSHIRE 1919. This simple stone war
memorial was designed to serve the village with water in perpetuity.

BELLINGHAM, NORTHUMBERLAND: 1902. Blood is thicker than water, but at Bellingham the two were brought together on the Boer War Memorial, which is also a drinking fountain. The wreathed canopy shelters a soldier in full South African kit complete with Lee Enfield.

KENSINGTON HIGH STREET: 1900. *Fin-de-siècle* elegance. This
elegant Baroque Portland stone monument was presented by
H. Wilson in 1900 to replace an earlier facility on the site.

above left ST. BOTOLPH'S, ALDGATE: 1903. This rather grotesque cast-iron cherub, astride a ewer and brandishing a paddle, sits on a plinth decorated with hideous dolphins' heads from which the water originally flowed. Unfortunately it offers little sustenance to those latter-day inebriates who gather in the churchyard to receive Christian charity.

above right ST BOTOLPH'S, ALDGATE: 1906. Refined classicism. This pedimented bay with its shell niche and contrasting sandstone rusticated pilasters recalls the benevolent life of Frederic David Mocatta, who died on 16 January 1905. Unusually the fountain retains its original cups and chains.

FINSBURY CIRCUS: 1904. Merry England. This whimsical little tiled pavilion provides shelter for a standard polished pink granite Association fountain beside the bowling green at Finsbury Circus in the heart of the City of London.

KENSINGTON GARDENS CHILDREN'S PLAYGROUND: 1909. Time
Flies. The crowning clock tower reminds those who drink beneath
of the transient pleasures of childhood. The fountain bears the
poignant inscription 'In memory of a Beloved son and of one who
loved little children 1909'.

NEWCASTLE-UPON-TYNE: HORATIO STREET: 1914. This fine horse
and cattle trough commemorates William Lisle Blenkinsopp
Coulson and 'his efforts to help the weak and defenceless among
mankind and in the animal world'. The bronze bust was designed
by Alexis Rudier. The original lions head spout is missing.

ACKNOWLEDGEMENTS

Although the author takes full responsibility for the opinions and views expressed in the book, various individuals have been most helpful and supportive. Special thanks are due to Liisa Davies, who typed the manuscript, and to Commander Randall of the Drinking Fountain Association, who gave me unrestricted access to the records.

The assistance of the following is also gratefully acknowledged: Hugh Davies, Jane Davies, Professor Paul Davies, Clive Smith, and the staffs of the British Architectural Library / RIBA, English Heritage, the Greater London Record Office and History Library, the National Monuments Record, *Punch* and the city libraries at Carlisle, Dudley, Durham and Newcastle-upon-Tyne.

·:·   ·:·   ·:·

All the photographs and illustrations are by the author or from the author's own collection with the exception of the following: p.46 (bottom): Greater London Record Office and History Library; p.47: Drinking Fountain Association; p.82: Dudley Public Library and Archives; p.84: Carlisle Public Library; pp.88 and 144: City Engineer, Newcastle-on-Tyne.